JOHN MI

CHALLENGE

CW01023900

THE PEAK DISTRICT -
THREE COUNTIES
CHALLENGE WALK

by

JOHN N. MERRILL

Maps and photographs by John N. Merrill

TRAIL CREST PUBLICATIONS Ltd.,
- "from footprint to finished book."

1993

Sandia Mountains
New Mexico. USA

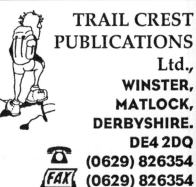

TRAIL CREST
PUBLICATIONS
Ltd.,
WINSTER,
MATLOCK,
DERBYSHIRE.
DE4 2DQ
☎ (0629) 826354
FAX (0629) 826354

Concieved, edited, typeset, designed, paged, printed, marketed and distributed by John N. Merrill.

© Text & walks - John N. Merrill 1993
© Maps & photographs - John N. Merrill 1993.

First Published - April 1993.

ISBN 0 874754 15 2

U.S.A.
office -
P.O.Box 124.
Santa Rosa,
New Mexico.
88435
U.S.A.

Please note - The maps in this guide are purely illustrative. You are encouraged to use the appropriate 1:25,000 O.S. map.

Meticulous research has been undertaken to ensure that this publication is highly accurate at the time of going to press. The publishers, however, cannot be held responsible for alterations, errors or omissions, but they would welcome notification of such for future editions.

Typeset in - Bookman bold, italic and plain 9pt and 18pt.

Printed by - John N. Merrill at Milne House, Speedwell Mill, Miller's Green, Wirksworth, Derbyshire. DE4 4BL

Cover sketchs by John Creber - Roaches, Three Shire Heads, Tittesworth Reservoir & Hen Cloud.
- © Trail Crest Publications Ltd. 1993.

An all British product.

The author on the summit of Mt.Taylor (11,301ft.), New Mexico.

ABOUT JOHN N. MERRILL

Born in the flatlands of Bedfordshire he soon moved to Sheffield and discovered the joy of the countryside in the Peak District, where he lives. A keen walker who travels the world exploring mountains and trails. Over the last twenty years he has walked more than 150,000 miles and worn out over sixty pairs of boots. He has written more than 120 walk guides to areas in Britain and abroad, and created numerous challenge walks which have been used to raise more than £500,000 for charity. New Mexico, USA is his second home.

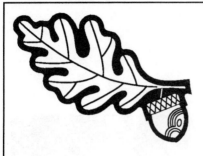

CONTENTS

Page No.

INTRODUCTION

I kept putting it off, but I don't really know - perhaps I was afraid to break the spell - but the walk was around my favourite area of the Peak District. I had had the idea in mind for several years but kept putting it aside. Then one day, I decided to do it at the weekend - the first day of "summer time"! That was a joke, it was cold and cloudy, but thankfully it never rained.

The plan was simple, to start from Tittesworth Reservoir and ascend the hills along the western side of the Peak District. And, to return via one of the highest inns and highest village in Britain. I was walking before 9.0 a.m. - no one about and I saw no other walker for three hours, until Shutlingsloe with a party of thirty on top! I pressed on to Tegg's Nose and to Lamaload Reservoir. I knew I was over half way but time was marching on and seven hours out I ascended Shining Tor. Now its downhill I thought! Onto the Cat & Fiddle and the descent to Three Shire Heads. Then it was ascending to Flash before the final miles back to the reservoir. With three bars of chocolate and a banana eaten all day. I entered the reservoir car park as dusk was approaching - 10 1/2 hours of non stop walking.

I leant against the car happy and exhilarated. I don't know why I waited so long to do it - its fantastic - one of my most rewarding days in the Peak for many a year. Although I knew the whole route from different walks I had never done it as a whole. I can only hope that you experience such a day on your circuit through the finest hills of the Peak District, that straddle the three counties of Staffordshire, Cheshire and Derbyshire; I know you are in for a truly exceptional day......

Happy walking!
John N. Merrill

Footslogger says - "an outstanding walk this - enjoy!"

Whilst every care is taken detailing and describing the walk in this book, it should be borne in mind that the countryside changes by the seasons and the work of man. I have described the walk to the best of my ability, detailing what I have found on the walk in the way of stiles and signs. Obviously with the passage of time stiles become broken or replaced by a ladder stile or even a small gate. Signs too have a habit of being broken or pushed over. All the route follow rights of way and only on rare occasions will you have to overcome obstacles in its path, such as a barbed wire fence or electric fence. On rare occasions rights of way are rerouted and these ammendments are included in the next edition.

The seasons bring occasional problems whilst out walking which should also be borne in mind. In the height of summer paths become overgrown and you will have to fight your way through in a few places. In low lying areas the fields are often full of crops, and although the pathline goes straight across it may be more practical to walk round the field edge to get to the next stile or gate. In summer the ground is generally dry but in autumn and winter, especially because of our climate, the surface can be decidedly wet and slippery; sometimes even gluttonous mud!

These comments are part of countryside walking which help to make your walk more interesting or briefly frustrating. Standing in a farmyard up to your ankles in mud might not be funny at the time but upon reflection was one of the highlights of the walk!

The mileage for each walk is based on three calculations -

1. pedometer reading.
2. the route map measured on the map.
3. the time I took for the walk.

I believe the figure stated for each walk to be very accurate but we all walk differently and not always in a straight line! The time allowed for each walk is on the generous side and does not include pub stops etc. The figure is based on the fact that on average a person walks 2 1/2 miles an hours but less in hilly terrain.

HOW TO DO IT

The whole walk is covered by the 1:25,000 Outdoor Leisure map - *The White Peak - west sheet.*

The walk is planned in a clockwise direction so that you do the hardest part first! There is a youth hostel at Meerbrook and another at Gradbach - both of which you pass; apart from that you are in high country with only the villages of Wildboarclough and Flash en route. The Cat and Fiddle Inn - third highest in England - is passed with two thirds of the route done. The car park at Tittesworth Reservoir closes at sunset. The vast majority of the route is along well defined paths - only the start and Flash area are they little used.

The aim is to complete in a day but with a back up party you can to it two halves by being met at Lamaload Reservoir or the Cat & Fiddle Inn. Back up parties can also monitor your progress by meeting you at the car parks at Gradbach, Tegg's Nose, Lamaload Reservoir and in Flash (no car park) before the final miles. It is a tough day with numerous "hills" to ascend. It is best to adopt a steady pace and keep it up all day - don't rush and burn yourself out. After the Cat & Fiddle Inn it is mostly flat or downhill, but with a few short ascents to Oliver Hill and to Adder's Green.

About 10 to 12 hours is needed to complete the route, but depends on how long you spend in the pubs along the way! Ideally it should be done in a day to get the full sense of achievement but this is not a criterion. You are quite happy to do it over a weekend or two day period - the aim is to encompass three counties in the Peak District. For the successful there is a special four colour embroidered green cloth badge and special certificate, from John Merrill at Trail Crest Publications Ltd. They also keep a master record of all the successful walkers. You are welcome to call in at the office/works at Wirksworth for your badge and learn of new challenges in the pipeline!

Footslogger says - "Don't rush - take your time - and enjoy the walk"

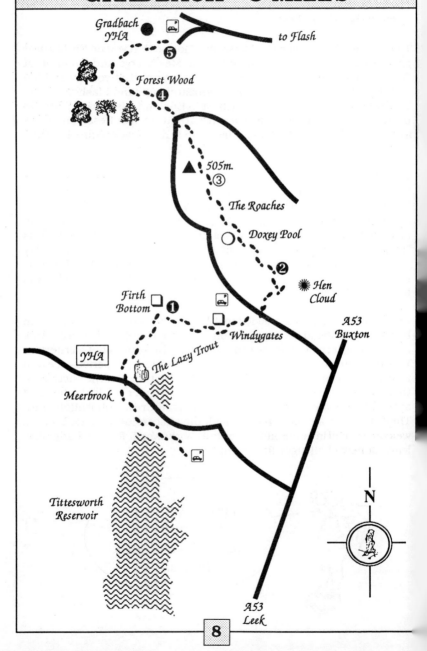

Gradbach YHA

to Flash

⑤

Forest Wood

④

▲ 505m.
③

The Roaches

Doxey Pool

②

✳ Hen Cloud

A53 Buxton

Firth Bottom ①

Windygates

YHA

The Lazy Trout

Meerbrook

Tittesworth Reservoir

N

A53 Leek

STAGE ONE - TITTESWORTH RESERVOIR TO GRADBACH - 5 MILES

- allow 2 hours.

- Tittesworth Reservoir - Meerbrook - Frith Bottom - Windygates - The Roaches - Doxey Pool - Trig Point 505m. - Forest Wood - River Dane - Gradbach Y.H.A.

- 1:25,000 Outdoor Leisure Map - The White Peak - West Sheet.

Tittesworth Reservoir. Beneath the Roaches. Gradbach.

- The Lazy Trout, Meerbrook. Refreshments at the Reservoir Amenity area.

ABOUT THE STAGE - Infront of you is the first "hill" - 2 miles to the ridge of The Roaches. The scenery is magnificent up there with an impressive battery of gritstone rock. You descend through Forest Wood to the River Dane, which you see more of later, and reach Gradbach ready for the next hill! You are in Staffordshire for the whole of this stage.

WALKING INSTRUCTIONS - Return to the road from the car park and turn left along it to Meerbrook, crossing the reservoir - a favourite bird watching area. Pass a Methodist chapel on your left and the Lazy Trout Inn on your right, and turn right before the Youth Hostel. Walk along with St. Michael's church on your left to a track and turn right. Follow it to Lower Lee Farm, keeping to the right of it, before keeping to the lefthand side of the field to a stile and onto another and a track. Turn right along it to Frith Bottom. Walk through the farm to a gate and turn left along the edge of the field to a stile. Here turn right keeping to the edge of the field to a stile and onto a stone footbridge. Turn left and ascend the field edge, guided by stiles to the farm and impressive house - Windygates. Walk through the farm and turn left up stone footpath steps and walk along the lefthand side of the field to a stile and road beneath The Roaches.

Go straight across and continue ascending for another 150 yards to where a path from your left joins yours - you are now in The Roaches Estate. Here turn left along it to a stile. Continue ahead on the path to the main overhanging gritstone crag. Walk beneath it before turning right and ascending to the crest of the crag. Turn left and gently ascend the spine of The Roaches to Doxey Pool and onto the trig point 505m. Behind you is Hen Cloud, which you walk beneath on your return! Continue on the path from the trig point and descend to the road, near Roach End. Turn right and descend the track for a few yards to a stile on your left. Continue descending with a wall on your right to a footpath sign and beech trees. Continue ahead descending at first then contouring round to your left - keeping to the upper path - as you walk through Forest Wood. In 1/2 mile reach the path junction for Gradbach. Continue ahead with the Black Brook on your right for 150 yards to a footbridge. Turn right across it and follow the path which soon turns left as you aim for Gradbach YHA with the River Dane on your left.

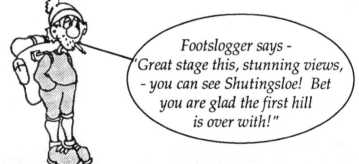

Footslogger says -
'Great stage this, stunning views,
- you can see Shutingsloe! Bet
you are glad the first hill
is over with!"

Meerbook YHA.

The Roaches - in winter.

Doxey Pool.

STAGE TWO -
GRADBACH TO LANGLEY
- 6 MILES
- allow 2 1/2 hours.

Gradbach YHA - River Dane - Bennettshitch - Hole Edge - A54 - Leech Wood - Wildboarclough - Shutlingsloe, 506m. - Macclesfield Forest - Trentabank Reservoir - Ridgegate Reservoir - Bottoms Reservoir - Langley.

 - 1:25,000 Outdoor Leisure Map - The White Peak - West Sheet.

 Gradbach. Trentabank Reservoir.

 - Leather Smithy, Ridgegate Reservoir.

ABOUT THE STAGE - Almost immediately you enter Cheshire and stay in the county for the whole stage. First you climb over moorland to reach Wildboarclough and the base of Shutlingsloe - the only true hill in the Peak District. Now you ascend to its summit for a magnificent view - over 27,000 people a year stand on this lofty summit. You descend through Macclesfield Forest to reservoirs and an inn, before the next hill! On the moors curlew and skylarks can be heard.

WALKING INSTRUCTIONS - Continue up the drive from the Youth Hostel and turn left down the road past the car park. Just after turn left over a footbridge and cross a field to a stile and road close to a bridge over the River Dane. Turn left along the road and enter Cheshire. On the other side turn right, as footpath signed, with a plaque and verse to "The Stroller". The path is well defined and angles up the hillside, past a quarry to the single laned road near Bennettshitch. Turn right along it past the farm and onto the next one, Hole-edge. Just past it turn left, as footpath signed, and follow a track to a solitary building. Follow the track around the right of it before it swings left. Continue on the path beneath the crest of the moorland, and in little over 1/2 mile gain the A54 road. Cross over to a stile and path sign and continue descending aiming for the righthand side of the field to gain a track with Leech Wood on your left. Reaching the road in Wildboarclough turn right and descend past Crag Hall on your right and onto St. Saviour church and impressive mill - a former post office.

At the road junction just afterwards turn left then right and ascend the farm road towards Banktop. Before the farm, as signed, turn left and begin ascending the fields, then open country, on a well defined path, and ascend the steep slope of Shutlingsloe to its summit. Continue down the otherside walking along a stone flagged path across the moors, via a footbridge, to Macclesfield Forest. Here you pick up the path signs - Trentabank. In the forest you follow a wide track and gradually descend to the road above Trentabank Reservoir and a car park on your left. Turn left along the road and soon right so as to walk beside Ridgegate Reservoir to the Leather Smithy Inn. Turn left and descend the road to Bottoms Reservoir and a row of cottages. Here you pick up the Gritstone Trail with Tegg's Nose ahead - part of your next stage!

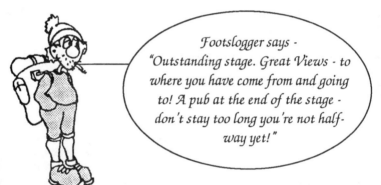

Footslogger says - "Outstanding stage. Great Views - to where you have come from and going to! A pub at the end of the stage - don't stay too long you're not half-way yet!"

Gradbach YHA - on New Year's Day!

Crag Hall, Wildboarclough & Shutlingsloe.

Bottoms Reservoir and Tegg's Nose.

STAGE THREE - LANGLEY TO LAMALOAD RESERVOIR - 4 MILES

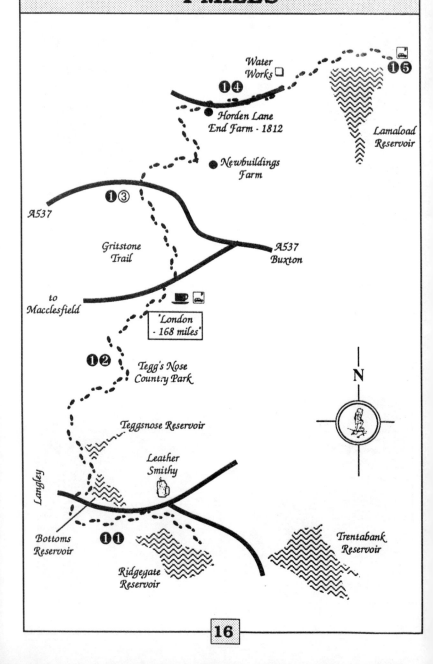

STAGE THREE -
LANGLEY TO LAMALOAD RESERVOIR
- 4 MILES

- allow 1 1/2 hours.

- Bottoms Reservoir - Teggsnose Reservoir - Gritstone Trail - Tegg's Nose Country Park - Windyway House - A537 - Higherlane Farm - Snipe House - Water Works - Lamaload Reservoir car park.

-1:25,000 Outdoor Leisure Map - The White Peak - West Sheet.

- Trentabank Reservoir. Tegg's Nose Country Park. Lamaload Reservoir.

Refreshments at Tegg's Nose car park.

ABOUT THE STAGE - For the first 2 1/2 miles you follow the Gritstone Trail as you ascend to Tegg's Nose and on towards Lamaload Reservoir. There are a few short ascents to get there, while on your left (westwards) are views over the Cheshire Plain. At Lamaload your are over half-way and at the base of the last major hill!

WALKING INSTRUCTIONS - Opposite Cottage No. 7 overlooking Bottoms Reservoir, turn right on the Gritstone Trail and walk around the reservoir to the steps and road before Teggsnose Reservoir. Cross this reservoir to a Gritstone Trail notice board and turn left and ascend the steps. Continue ascending to Tegg's Nose.Gaining the track at the top turn right and keep to the righthand side of the quarry as you walk through the country park and past the quarry machinery to a gate. Turn right and continue on the path to the road and entrance to Tegg's Nose car park - teas here. Also pass a stone milepost - *London 168 miles.*

Continue up the road a few yards from the car park and opposite Windyway House Turn left, as Gritstone Trail signed and stiled, and ascend the fields, guided by stiles. Descend the other side to a ladder stile and onto the A537, reached via stone steps. Turn left then right to the entrance of Bull Hill road. A few yards down it is the stile and footpath sign. Turn right and descend the field and ascend the other side to a ladder stile. Continue to a stile and keep the wall on your left to gain another. Here the Gritstone Trail turns left; you keep straight ahead on the farm track to Newbuildings Farm to a stile on your left in a few yards. Here turn left and descend to the righthand corner of the field to a ladder stile. Continue descending, guided by stiles, keeping to the left of Horden Lane End Farm, built in 1812. Here gain the water board road. Turn right and follow it past Higherlane Farm and Snipe House, before it descends towards the works at the base of Lamaload Reservoir. Turn right just before the gates and follow the path around the works on your left to the second path sign. Here turn right and ascend to the reservoir on your right. Continue on a good path and descend to the car park at Lamaload Reservoir.

Footslogger says - "Nice hilly route with Shining Tor ahead! At least you are now over half-way! Great cup of tea at Tegg's Nose."

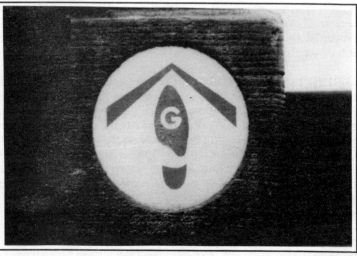

Gritstone Trail sign.

Quarry machinery - Tegg's Nose.

John Merrill walkers on the summit of Shutlingsloe.

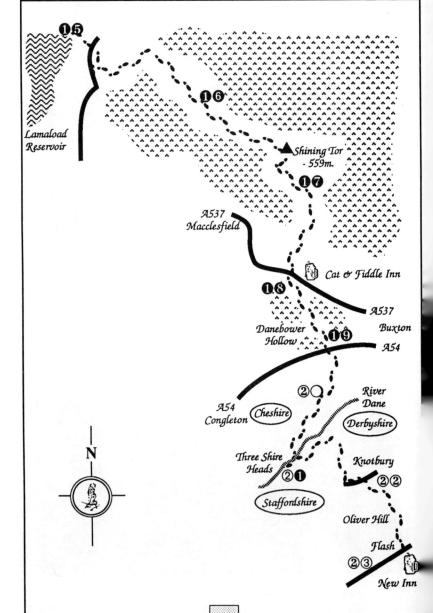

STAGE FOUR - LAMALOAD RESERVOIR TO FLASH - 8 MILES

15

Lamaload Reservoir

16

▲ Shining Tor - 559m.

17

A537 Macclesfield

Cat & Fiddle Inn

18

A537 Buxton

Danebower Hollow

19

A54

A54 Congleton

Cheshire

20

River Dane

Derbyshire

Three Shire Heads

21

Staffordshire

Knotbury

22

Oliver Hill

Flash

23

New Inn

N

STAGE FOUR -
LAMALOAD
RESERVOIR
TO FLASH
- 8 MILES
- allow 3 hours.

- Lamaload Reservoir Car Park - Shining Tor, 559m.
- Cat & Fiddle Inn - Danebower Hollow - Three Shire Heads -
Knotbury - Wolf Edge - Oliver Hill - Flash.

1:25,000 Outdoor Leisure map - The White Peak - West Sheet.

- Lamaload Reservoir. Opposite Cat & Fiddle Inn.

- Cat & Fiddle Inn. New Inn, Flash.

ABOUT THE STAGE - The highest part of the route, with Shining Tor 559m. The Cat & Fiddle Inn is the third highest in the country, while Flash at 1,518 ft. is the highest village in England. You start in Cheshire and at Three Shire Heads step briefly into Derbyshire before entering Staffordshire, where you stay for the rest of the walk. Outstanding moorland countryside most of the way with the convergence of packhorse routes at Three Shire Heads; a stage to savour.

WALKING INSTRUCTIONS - From the car park at Lamaload Reservoir gain the road and turn right. In less than 1/4 mile turn left, as footpath signed - Shining Tor. The post has a memorial plaque to Jack & Mary Gyte. The well defined path keeps to the left of a small forest before swinging right and ascending moorland to the crest of the slope. From here you can see Shining Tor as you walk along the crest to its slopes. Here cross a stile and ascend with a wall on your right to the left of the trig point. Here gain a wide path and turn right passing the trig point - reached via a ladder stile - before swinging left beside the wall on your right to the path from Shooter's Clough. Turn right on the good path/track to a ladder stile and onto the A537 near the Cat & Fiddle Inn. Just before the road pass another stone milepost - *London 164 miles. Macclesfield 6 miles.* Turn left to the inn.

Opposite the inn turn right and follow the wide track over the moorland. In over 1/2 mile pass the path on your right down Cumberland Clough. Continue on the path and descend gently down Danebower Hollow to the A54 road. Go straight across, as path signed, and descend steeply past a solitary chimney on your right to the path beside the infant River Dane on your left. You basically keep the river on your left for the next 3/4 mile to the packhorse bridges at Three Shire Heads. The path is not always defined but all the stiles are there. At the packhorse bridge cross the River Dane and enter Derbyshire. Go through a gate and ascend the track for less than 1/4 mile to the first track on your right. Here turn right and enter Staffordshire and follow the track round to your left to a junction. Turn right and pass the houses of Knotbury to another T junction. Turn left and in a few yards turn right and cross the magnificent single stone slabbed footbridge and ascend to the top of Wolf Edge, keeping a wall on your right. Cross the rocks at the top to a stile and on to another. Here bear right along a track but after two fields leave it on your left and cross the stiled fields to the lane on the outskirts of Flash. Turn left to the New Inn in Flash.

Footslogger says -
"Great stage this, it's nearly all down hill now after Shining Tor. Great drink at the Cat & Fiddle!

Milepost - "To London 164 miles."

Cat & Fiddle Inn.

Three Shire Heads.

STAGE FIVE - FLASH TO TITTESWORTH RESERVOIR - 5 MILES

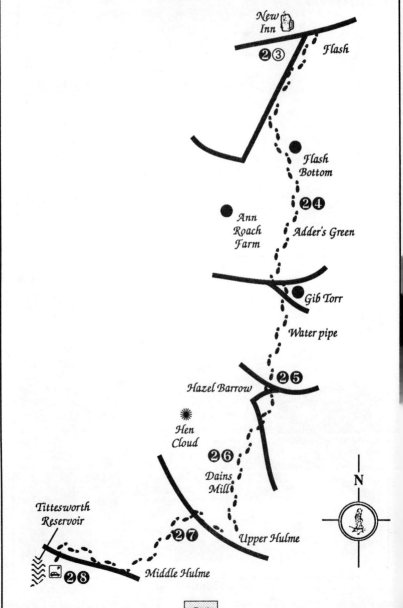

turn left and walk along the high ground to some gritstone outcrops to a stile. Continue now on a track to the road near Hazel Barrow at Corner House.

Keep straight ahead on the road and keep to the lefthand on in less than 1/4 mile. Pass the house "Eleven Steps" and just after turn right through the gate and track to Misty Hill. Keep to the right of the farm, as signed, and reach a stile. Descend to a footbridge and stile below Summerhill. Keep to the right of the stream before maintaining height to two more stiles, with Ferny Knowl on your left. Here gain a track and descend to another. Turn left then right at a stile and continue close to the stream on your left to the ruins of Dains Mill. Follow the track round and down to Upper Hulme. Continue ahead on the road through the works complex and follow the road round to your right to a farm track. Turn left down it but, as guided by stiles and signs keep to the right of it before reaching the lefthand side of the field beyond the farm. Continue along the lefthand side to a stile and footbridge. Continue to a track and descend this to the road beside Middle Hulme. Here turn right and walk along the road to the car park little over 1/4 mile away.

Footslogger says -
"Well done. I know its been a hard walk and your legs ache, but what a circuit in the three counties? I've enjoyed your company and hope to see you again soon - Happy Hiking! Now for a steak, strawberries and a hot bath!"

The Roaches.

The Roaches & Hen Cloud from near Tittesworth Reservoir.

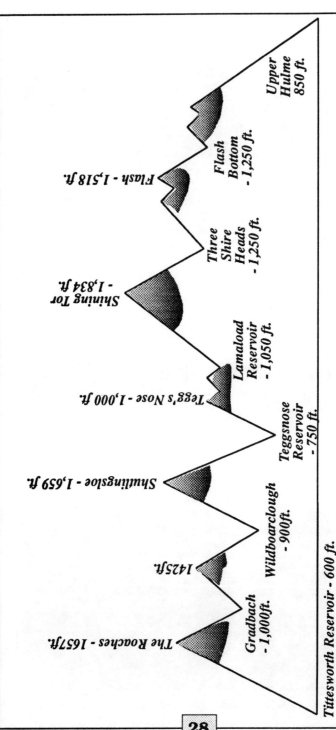

The Roaches - 1657ft.

Gradbach - 1,000ft.

1425ft.

Wildboarclough - 900ft.

Shutlingsloe - 1,659 ft.

Teggsnose Reservoir - 750 ft.

Tegg's Nose - 1,000 ft.

Lamaload Reservoir - 1,050 ft.

Shining Tor - 1,834 ft.

Three Shire Heads - 1,250 ft.

Flash - 1,518 ft.

Flash Bottom - 1,250 ft.

Upper Hulme 850 ft.

Tittesworth Reservoir - 600 ft.

TRAIL PROFILE - approx 4,800 ft. of ascent & descent over 28 miles

AMENITIES GUIDE -

 ## INNS - passed en route -

The Lazy Trout, Meerbrook.
Leather Smithy, Langley.
Cat & Fiddle Inn.
New Inn, Flash.

Teas -

Tittesworth Reservoir
Tegg's Nose Country Park.

YHA

Meerbrook - Old School, Meerbrook, Leek.
Staffs. ST13 8SJ
Tel. 053834 - 244

Gradbach Mill - Gradbach, Quarnford, Buxton,
Derbyshire. SK17 0SU
Tel. 0260 - 227625

WEATHERCALL - 0898 500 411

Camping - Gradbach.

Bed & Breakfast - a random selection -

Langley - Mrs. M. Birch, High Low Farm, Langley, Macclesfield.
SK11 0NE

Upper Hulme - Jacky Wildman, Roaches House, Leek, ST13
8TZ

Many places off the route in Leek, Macclesfield and Buxton.

LOG

DATE & Time STARTED...

DATE & Time COMPLETED..

ROUTE POINT	MILE NO.	ARR.	DEP.	COMMENTS WEATHER
Tittesworth Reservoir	0			
The Roaches	2			
Forest Wood	4			
Gradbach	5			
Leech Wood	7			
Shutlingsloe	8.5			
Bottoms Reservoir	11			
Tegg's Nose	12			
Lamaload Reservoir	15			
Shining Tor 569m.	17			
Three Shire Heads	21			
Flash	23			
Gib Torr	24.5			
Dains Mill	26			
Tittesworth Res,	28			

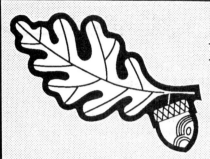

JOHN MERRILL'S PEAK DISTRICT

THREE COUNTIES CHALLENGE WALK

Badges measure 3 1/2" wide by 3" high and are a green cloth with brown, black, yellow and white embroidery.

BADGE ORDER FORM

Date completed ....

Time ....

Name...

Address ....

....

Price - £2.75 each including postage, VAT and signed certificate.

"I've done a John Merrill Walk" T shirt - Emerald Green with white lettering - all sizes - £7.50 including postage and VAT.
JOHN MERRILL'S HAPPY WALKING CAP - £2.50

From - Trail Crest Publications Ltd., Winster, Matlock, Derbyshire. DE4 2DQ

☎ 0629 - 826354

.... **You may photocopy this form if needed** ....

THE JOHN MERRILL CHALLENGE WALK BADGE - walk this route twice or complete another of John Merrill's Challenge Walks and send details and cheque for £2.75 for a special 2 challenge walk circular four colour embroidered badge, to Trail Crest Publications; Ltd. price includes postage and VAT.

OTHER CHALLENGE WALKS BY JOHN N. MERRILL

DAY CHALLENGES -

John Merrill's White Peak Challenge Walk - 25 miles.
Circular walk from Bakewell involving 3,600 feet of ascent.

John Merrill's Dark Peak Challenge Walk - 24 miles.
Circular walk from Hathersage involving 3,300 feet of ascent.

**John Merrill's Staffordshire Moorlands Challenge Walk
- 26 miles.** Circular walk from Oakamoor involving 2,200 feet of ascent.

John Merrill's Yorkshire Dales Challenge Walk - 23 miles.
Circular walk from Kettlewell involving 3,600 feet of ascent.

John Merrill's North Yorkshire Moors Challenge Walk - 24 miles.
Circular walk from Goathland - a seaside bash - involving 2,000 feet of ascent.

The Little John Challenge Walk - 28 miles.
Circular walk from Edwinstowe in Sherwood Forest - Robin Hood
country.

Peak District End to End Walks.
1. Gritstone Edge Walk - 23 miles down the eastern edge system.
2. Limestone Dale Walk - 24 miles down the limestone dales from
Buxton to Ashbourne.

The Rutland Water Challenge walk - 24 miles
Around the shore of Rutland Water, the largest man made reservoir in Britain.

The Malvern Hills Challenge Walk - 20 miles.
Beneath and along the crest of the Malvern Hills.

The Salter's Way - 25 miles.
Across Cheshire from Northwich to the Pennines, following an old salt way.

John Merrill's Snowdon Challenge Walk - 30 miles.
A tough day walk involving 5,000 feet of ascent and descent from the sea to the
summit of Snowdon AND BACK!

John Merrill's Charnwood Forest Challenge Walk - 25 miles
The grandslam of this area of north Leicestershire, starting from Bradgate Park, taking in several hill's and monastic buildings, involving 1,600 feet of ascent and descent

John Merrill's Three Counties Challenge Walk. - 28 miles
Magnificent tough walk around the "hills" of western Peakland, straddling the counties of Staffordshire, Cheshire & Derbyshire. 4,800 feet of ascent.

Forthcoming titles -
The Quantock's Way.

MULTIPLE DAY CHALLENGE WALKS -

The Limey Way - 40 miles
Down twenty limestone dales from Castleton to Thorpe in the Peak District in eight stages, starting and ending at Ashbourne. The finest longest distance walk in the Peak! Taking in the grandest and highest sights.

The River's Way - 43 miles.
Down the five main river systems of the Peak District, from Edale, the end of the Pennine Way, to Ilam.

The Peakland Way - 96 miles.
John Merrill's classic walk around the Peak District National Park, starting and finishing at Ashbourne. The route of eight stages takes in the variety of the Park - limestone dales, gritstone moorland, gritstone edges , historic buildings and trails. A route combing the finest assets the Peak District has. More than 7,000 people have walked the entire route since it was inugurated in 1974.

Peak District Hiqh Level Route - 90 miles
Clrcular walk from Matlock taking in the highest and remotest parts of the Peak District.

COASTAL WALKS & NATIONAL TRAILS -

The Cleveland Way - 112 miles around the North Yorkshire Moors and coast - a truly exceptional walk.

The lsle of Wight Coast Path - 77 miles.
Complete encirclement of a magnificent island.

Forthcoming titles -
Walking Angelsey's coastline.
The Pembrokeshire Coast Path.
The Ridgeway

The Pilgrim's Way
The North Downs Way
The South Downs Way

Offa's Dyke Path

"from footprint to finished book"

CIRCULAR WALK GUIDES -
SHORT CIRCULAR WALKS IN THE PEAK DISTRICT - Vol. 1 and 2
CIRCULAR WALKS IN WESTERN PEAKLAND
SHORT CIRCULAR WALKS IN THE STAFFORDSHIRE MOORLANDS
SHORT CIRCULAR WALKS - TOWNS & VILLAGES OF THE PEAK DISTRICT
SHORT CIRCULAR WALKS AROUND MATLOCK
SHORT CIRCULAR WALKS IN THE DUKERIES
SHORT CIRCULAR WALKS IN SOUTH YORKSHIRE
SHORT CIRCULAR WALKS IN SOUTH DERBYSHIRE
SHORT CIRCULAR WALKS AROUND BUXTON
SHORT CIRCULAR WALKS AROUND WIRKSWORTH
SHORT CIRCULAR WALKS IN THE HOPE VALLEY
40 SHORT CIRCULAR WALKS IN THE PEAK DISTRICT
CIRCULAR WALKS ON KINDER & BLEAKLOW
SHORT CIRCULAR WALKS IN SOUTH NOTTINGHAMSHIRE
SHIRT CIRCULAR WALKS IN CHESHIRE
SHORT CIRCULAR WALKS IN WEST YORKSHIRE
CIRCULAR WALKS TO PEAK DISTRICT AIRCRAFT WRECKS by John Mason
CIRCULAR WALKS IN THE DERBYSHIRE DALES
SHORT CIRCULAR WALKS IN EAST DEVON
SHORT CIRCULAR WALKS AROUND HARROGATE
SHORT CIRCULAR WALKS IN CHARNWOOD FOREST
SHORT CIRCULAR WALKS AROUND CHESTERFIELD
SHORT CIRCULAR WALKS IN THE YORKS DALES - Vol 1 - Southern area.
LONG CIRCULAR WALKS IN THE PEAK DISTRICT - Vol.1 and 2.
LONG CIRCULAR WALKS IN THE STAFFORDSHIRE MOORLANDS
LONG CIRCULAR WALKS IN CHESHIRE
WALKING THE TISSINGTON TRAIL
WALKING THE HIGH PEAK TRAIL

CANAL WALKS -
VOL 1 - DERBYSHIRE & NOTTINGHAMSHIRE
VOL 2 - CHESHIRE & STAFFORDSHIRE
VOL 3 - STAFFORDSHIRE
VOL 4 - THE CHESHIRE RING
VOL 5 - LINCOLNSHIRE & NOTTINGHAMSHIRE
VOL 6 - SOUTH YORKSHIRE
VOL 7 - THE TRENT & MERSEY CANAL

JOHN MERRILL DAY CHALLENGE WALKS -
WHITE PEAK CHALLENGE WALK
DARK PEAK CHALLENGE WALK
PEAK DISTRICT END TO END WALKS
STAFFORDSHIRE MOORLANDS CHALLENGE WALK
THE LITTLE JOHN CHALLENGE WALK
YORKSHIRE DALES CHALLENGE WALK
NORTH YORKSHIRE MOORS CHALLENGE WALK

LAKELAND CHALLENGE WALK
THE RUTLAND WATER CHALLENGE WALK
MALVERN HILLS CHALLENGE WALK
THE SALTER'S WAY
THE SNOWDON CHALLENGE
CHARNWOOD FOREST CHALLENGE WALK
THREE COUNTIES CHALLENGE WALK (Peak District).

INSTRUCTION & RECORD -
HIKE TO BE FIT.....STROLLING WITH JOHN
THE JOHN MERRILL WALK RECORD BOOK

MULTIPLE DAY WALKS -
THE RIVERS'S WAY
PEAK DISTRICT: HIGH LEVEL ROUTE
PEAK DISTRICT MARATHONS
THE LIMEY WAY
THE PEAKLAND WAY

COAST WALKS & NATIONAL TRAILS -
ISLE OF WIGHT COAST PATH
PEMBROKESHIRE COAST PATH
THE CLEVELAND WAY

PEAK DISTRICT HISTORICAL GUIDES -
A to Z GUIDE OF THE PEAK DISTRICT
DERBYSHIRE INNS - an A to Z guide
HALLS AND CASTLES OF THE PEAK DISTRICT & DERBYSHIRE
TOURING THE PEAK DISTRICT & DERBYSHIRE BY CAR
DERBYSHIRE FOLKLORE
PUNISHMENT IN DERBYSHIRE
CUSTOMS OF THE PEAK DISTRICT & DERBYSHIRE
WINSTER - a souvenir guide
ARKWRIGHT OF CROMFORD
LEGENDS OF DERBYSHIRE
TALES FROM THE MINES by Geoffrey Carr
PEAK DISTRICT PLACE NAMES by Martin Spray

JOHN MERRILL'S MAJOR WALKS -
TURN RIGHT AT LAND'S END
WITH MUSTARD ON MY BACK
TURN RIGHT AT DEATH VALLEY
EMERALD COAST WALK

SKETCH BOOKS -
SKETCHES OF THE PEAK DISTRICT

for a free copy
of the
**John Merrill
Walk Guide**
Catalogue
write to -
Trail Crest Publications Ltd.,
Milne House, Speedwell Mill,
Miller's Green, Wirksworth,
Derbyshire. DE4 4BL

OVERSEAS GUIDES -
HIKING IN NEW MEXICO - Vol I - The Sandia and Manzano Mountains.
Vol 2 - Hiking "Billy the Kid" Country.
"WALKING IN DRACULA COUNTRY" - Romania.
IN PREPARATION -
SHORT CIRCULAR WALKS IN EAST STAFFORDSHIRE
SHORT CIRCULAR WALKS IN THE AMBER VALLEY (DERBYSHIRE).

THE HIKER'S CODE

✿ **Hike only along marked routes - do not leave the trail.**

✿ **Use stiles to climb fences; close gates.**

✿ **Camp only in designated campsites.**

✿ **Carry a light-weight stove.**

✿ **Leave the trail cleaner than you found it.**

✿ **Leave flowers and plants for others to enjoy.**

✿ **Keep dogs on a leash.**

✿ **Protect and do not disturb wildlife.**

✿ **Use the trail at your own risk.**

✿ **Leave only your thanks and footprints - take nothing but photographs.**